I0200704

This book belongs to

....

Written by Deborah Hassett
Illustrated by Sunshine

First Published 2019

© 2019 Deborahe Hassett

No part of this printed of video publication may be
reproduced, stored in or introduced into retrieval system,
or transmitted, in any form, or by any means (electrical,
mechanical, photocopying, recording or otherwise) without
the prior written permission of the author and copyright
owner: Deborah Hassett.

Alice's

Journey

By Deborah Hassett

Pictures By Sunshine

Alice skipped along,

not realizing the direction she was heading.

Sorrow wrapped her arms around her and together they ventured further into the forest.

Pain and Hurt soon joined them

until they were at Anguishes door.

Chaos invited them in

and they all sat down at the table
laid out by Self Doubt and Loathing.

Alice didn't realize the time she had spent with her new found friends.

She acknowledged that perhaps
she would return to Hope and Joy
who would be worried about her.

She excused herself and started for the door.

"You'll be back soon," called out Self Doubt and Sorrow.

"Perhaps" Alice replied. "But I won't be staying as long."

Love is waiting for me,
and she and I will be very busy.

I will have little time for you."

Alice made her way back through the forest and met Forgiveness.

They held hands

and followed the path to Family and Friendship.

Wonder and New Beginnings greeted her.

She was where she wanted to be.

Sometimes Sorrow and Pain came for a visit.

-KNOCK-

-KNOCK-

Alice, with Comfort and Love,

would spend time with them,

then send them away with a bag of hugs.

The
End.

www.ingramcontent.com/pod-product-compliance
Lightning Source LLC
Chambersburg PA
CBHW081228020426
42331CB00011B/2994